KING HENRY VIII

A Life from Beginning to End

Copyright © 2019 by Hourly History.

All rights reserved.

Table of Contents

Introduction
Early Life and Exile
The Battle for the Throne
The Tudor Dynasty Begins
England and Spain Join Forces
The Work of Henry VII
Late Life and Death
Conclusion

Introduction

In 1485, Henry VII became the first Tudor to ascend the throne of England, and in doing so, he established a royal dynasty which would last for more than a hundred years. Best known for ending the Wars of the Roses, the bloody civil wars fought between two rival branches of the House of Plantagenet for a good part of the fifteenth century, Henry VII's path to the crown was not an easy one to travel. In the end, Henry became the last English king to win his crown on the battlefield when he and his troops defeated and killed King Richard III at the Battle of Bosworth Field.

Henry did a lot for the British economy during his time as monarch. Instead of spending lavishly as some of his predecessors had done, Henry focused his attention on building new sources of revenue for his country. He also played a big role in bringing back power to the monarchy. The Wars of the Roses were born out of a lack of stability within the royal government from the time that Henry VI sat on the throne. Henry VII was able to reestablish the monarchy as a powerful and stable leadership entity, and although his reign did not come without discord and challenges, the people of England started seeing the monarchy as the seat of authority once again.

England's government underwent considerable modernization when Henry was in power. The legal system, in particular, was drastically changed to counteract corruption and, more importantly, thwart any attempts of rebellion against Henry's rule. Through these changes, the king was able to weaken the power of the nobles and swiftly deal with any threats to royal authority.

During his 23-year-long reign, Henry ended the dynastic wars that had plagued his country for decades, he established the Tudor family as the ruling dynasty, and he successfully rebuilt England's economy. Whether or not he was a good king has been debated by many, but Henry VII did prove successful in many of his endeavors.

Chapter One

Early Life and Exile

"Jasper earl of Pembroke returned into Wales to his earldom, where he found Henry, son to his brother Edmund earl of Richmond . . . kept as prisoner, but honorably brought up with the wife of William Herbert."

—Polydore Vergil

Henry VII was born to his mother, Margaret Beaufort, on January 28, 1457, at Pembroke Castle in Wales. Margaret was only 13 years old at the time of Henry's birth; her husband, Edmund Tudor, was not at her side since he had died just three months earlier.

Edmund Tudor, the earl of Richmond, was the half-brother of King Henry VI. Henry VI had chosen Margaret to become Edmund's wife in 1455 when Edmund was 24 years old and Margaret merely 12. Edmund and Margaret were both descendants of the House of Lancaster, which was one of the two branches of the royal House of Plantagenet. When the Wars of the Roses broke out in 1455, the House of Lancaster was set to fight against the other Plantagenet branch, the House of York, for the claim to the English throne. The symbols of the two houses—the Red Rose of Lancaster and the White Rose of York—gave name to these civil wars which would ravage England for the next three decades.

One year into the conflict, Edmund Tudor was sent to South Wales to enforce the reigning King Henry VI's authority. It was the summer of 1456, and an opposer had taken the castles at Carmarthen, Aberystwyth, and Carreg Cennen. By August, Edmund and his men had put down the rebellion and secured the castles for the king. However, while Edmund was away, Henry VI and one of the most powerful men in England, Richard of York, had been feuding—a feud which ended in Richard's dismissal. Richard was so furious that he sent 2,000 men under the direction of William Herbert to take South Wales. When Herbert and his men arrived at Carmarthen Castle, they encountered Edmund Tudor, and after capturing the castle, they left him imprisoned in the stronghold. Edmund would eventually die there in November of 1456 from bubonic plague.

As Edmund died while his wife was pregnant, his younger brother was tasked with watching over the widowed mother-to-be. Jasper Tudor, the earl of Pembroke, provided protection for Margaret while she was pregnant and made sure she was cared for during and after the delivery of Henry. Because of Margaret's young age, the birth was particularly difficult, and even though Margaret remarried in 1458, she would not have any more children. Margaret's new marriage meant that Henry would see little of his mother during his formative years; instead, he was brought up in Jasper's household by nurses and tutors. Among these servants was a woman named Jane ap Hywel. She eventually became Henry's governess and was most likely the one who taught him the Welsh language.

Jasper Tudor acted as a kind of stand-in father to Henry until 1461 when he and other nobles loyal to Henry VI and the House of Lancaster were defeated at the Battle of Mortimer's Cross. Their Yorkist opponents celebrated their victory by crowning the first Yorkist king, Edward IV, in March. When that happened, Jasper Tudor went into exile abroad. After he left, William Herbert, a Yorkist, took control over Pembroke Castle and four-year-old Henry. Eventually, Herbert was named the new earl of Pembroke. Some have suggested that Herbert might have been involved in a plot to murder Henry's father, Edmund. Herbert had, after all, been instrumental in the capture and imprisonment of Edmund Tudor at Carmarthen Castle where he died—that much is known. Then, just years later, he managed to supplant Edmund's brother at Pembroke and take charge of Edmund's young son.

Keeping Henry under his sway would no doubt be advantageous to Herbert since Henry was the rightful earl of Richmond and would inherit all the estates and powers associated with that title once he came of age. Herbert sought to gain a measure of control over these assets by having Henry marry one of his daughters. With this aim in mind, Herbert sent Henry to be raised with his own children at Raglan Castle under the watchful eye of his wife, Anne Devereux. For the next eight years, Anne became the new mother figure in Henry's life. She made sure that he received a proper education and was well cared for. Henry quickly became attached to Anne, and she would have a place in his heart for the rest of his life. The same was true for Anne and Herbert's children, many of whom would become lifelong friends to Henry. These childhood connections would come to play a pivotal role in the years leading to Henry's accession to the throne.

Herbert's plan to have one of his daughters marry Henry would not come to fruition, however, as these were tumultuous times in England. Edward IV had managed to stay in control this far, but his support among the leading families of England was waning, and the Lancastrians had no plans of giving up their claim to the throne. There were a number of uprisings and revolts in the north during this time, but all were suppressed by Yorkist armies. Meanwhile, Edward was in conflict with one of his leading advisers, Richard Neville, otherwise known as "Warwick the Kingmaker." Edward and Warwick were primarily at odds over the king's choice of a bride.

In 1464, Edward had secretly married Elizabeth Woodville—a match which did little to strengthen his claim to the throne and which humiliated Warwick, who had been busy negotiating a possible union with the daughter of the king of France. Edward's marriage to Elizabeth enraged Warwick to the point of rebellion. In 1467, he made an attempt to oust Edward from the throne with the help of Edward's little brother, George. It did not work, however, as the nobility would not get behind the plan. Warwick had to form another plan.

In 1469, this man, the Kingmaker who had been instrumental in installing Edward on the throne in the first place, defected from the Yorkist faction and joined the Lancastrians. Warwick's change of heart would have an unexpectedly large impact on 12-year-old Henry's life as his guardian, William Herbert, immediately sprung into action to bring Warwick down. Opposing Warwick would not prove easy, and when Herbert faced down with Warwick's rebels at the Battle of Edgecote Moor in July, Herbert and his men were soundly defeated. After the battle was over, both Herbert and his brother were captured and swiftly executed by the Lancastrians.

Henry, who had been present on the battlefield, was ushered to the safety of Weobley Castle where he spent the next few weeks with Herbert's widow, Anne Devereux. With his guardian dead, young Henry was left in quite a precarious situation. Luckily, the very next year, Warwick managed to restore Henry VI to the throne, and with the Lancastrians back in power, Henry's uncle Jasper Tudor was finally able to return from his exile abroad. When Jasper came back to court, he brought young Henry with him. Here, Henry was for the first time introduced to the king and allowed to see the inner workings of the royal government. Henry then accompanied Jasper on a mission to rally support for the king in the Yorkist areas of Wales.

However, Henry VI and the Lancastrians' time back in power would be shortlived. In the spring of 1471, Edward IV returned to England and reclaimed London as his own. Warwick was killed in battle shortly thereafter, and Henry VI was deposed and locked in the Tower of London only to be murdered a few weeks later. The Lancastrians scrambled to fight back against the Yorkists, but their efforts would come to nothing. With Henry VI dead and his son and sole heir killed in battle on May 4, the Lancastrians were left leaderless. Jasper and Henry, who had been raising an army in Wales, realized that the battle had been lost. It was time to cut their losses.

By this point, Henry Tudor was one of only two adult Lancastrian heirs not yet dead or imprisoned. This put him in a very dangerous position. Edward IV and his men were on a mission to extinguish any threat to Yorkist rule, and Henry was, in the words of historian Polydore Vergil, "the only imp now left of Henry VI's blood." After a daring escape during which Henry and Jasper managed to slip the grasp of Edward IV's men, the two Tudors set out on a ship heading to France. The wind would not blow in their favor, however, and after they were nearly shipwrecked by vicious storms, they washed up on the shore of Brittany in mid-September 1471.

Brittany was during this time an independent nation and almost constantly at war with France. Its leader, Duke Francis II, was a courteous host and treated Henry and Jasper "very handsomely for prisoners," but they were nonetheless very much at his mercy. Both France and England were keen to get their hands on the Tudors, and the pair were often used as political pawns during negotiations between Brittany, England, and France in the following years.

By 1476, Henry Tudor was the only adult Lancastrian heir still left in play, and Edward IV was desperate to lay his hands on him. After months of discussion, Edward was finally able to convince Duke Francis to hand over Henry on the condition that he would not come to harm. In November, English ships were waiting in the waters off the Breton coast, eager to take Henry Tudor into custody. But as he was being led to the port and almost certainly to his death, Henry suddenly fell ill. He quickly retreated to a nearby church to recover, and during this delay, Duke

Francis changed his mind. Whether the illness was real or feigned, Henry was safe, at least for now.

Meanwhile in England, Henry's mother Margaret was doing her part to protect her son's future. A shrewd and intelligent woman, Margaret had chosen a more conciliatory route to navigate the turmoil of the Wars of the Roses. After her husband died in 1471, Margaret quickly remarried to Thomas Stanley, a powerful and well-connected nobleman in the Yorkist court. Throughout the 1470s, Stanley and Margaret developed a close relationship with Edward IV's inner circle, with Margaret even being chosen as godmother to one of the king's daughters.

By 1482, Margaret had managed to secure a royal pardon for Henry for his part in the rebellion against Edward IV. She had also secured Henry's birthright, the earldom of Richmond with all its estates, as well as a portion of her own mother's vast estates. Henry was set to inherit all of his on the condition that he return to England "to be in the grace and favour of the king's highness." There was also talk of a possible betrothal between Henry and one of the king's daughters.

The stage was set for Henry's peaceful return to his home country, which he had left over a decade ago. But before these plans could come to fruition, disaster struck once again.

Chapter Two

The Battle for the Throne

"Henry Tudor and others, the King's Rebels and Traitors aforesaid, have intended at their coming, if they were in power, to do the most cruel murders, slaughters, robberies and disinheritances that were ever seen in any Christian realm."

—Richard III of England

In April of 1483, Edward IV died from an unknown illness at age 40. He left the kingdom to his 12-year-old son, Edward V, and his brother, Richard, who was supposed to act as regent until Edward V was old enough to rule by himself. However, Richard coveted the throne for himself and successfully claimed the seat of power in June when he was crowned King Richard III. Around the same time, Edward V and his younger brother were sent to live in the Tower of London where they mysteriously disappeared. Although the two brothers' fate cannot be known for certain, most historians agree that they were likely killed on the orders of their uncle, Richard III.

Meanwhile, Margaret started planting the seed that her son should replace Richard III as the king of England. Many were unhappy with Richard's ascent to power; even Yorkist supporters did not appreciate his ousting of his two nephews. Seizing the opportunity, Margaret started plotting with Edward IV's widow to overthrow Richard. As part of the plan, they agreed upon a betrothal between Henry and Edward's eldest daughter, Elizabeth of York. A union between Henry and Elizabeth would bring the Lancastrians and Yorkists together under the same banner, Margaret reasoned. This way, Margaret hoped to rally widespread support for Henry's accession to the throne. She and her son would need it.

In normal circumstances, few would have considered Henry Tudor an heir to the throne. Although his father was a half-brother of Henry VI, they did not share the same father, so Henry was not a descendent of Henry V. Henry's main claim to the throne was derived from his mother, Margaret Beaufort, who was the great-great granddaughter of Edward III. Thus, through Margaret, Henry had a small measure of Plantagenet blood in his veins. This was hardly a strong dynastic claim to the throne, and the fact that Henry had spent almost all of his life locked away in castles or exiled in Brittany made him virtually unknown to most people in England. Yet the situation in England was desperate—due to the Wars of the Roses, there were not many potential heirs left.

By the end of 1483, Henry pledged to marry Elizabeth of York in an effort to rally support from the Yorkist faction. Meanwhile, Richard III was dealing with a major rebellion against his rule. Amongst the rebels were of course Lancastrians but also disaffected Yorkists who had been loyal to Edward IV and Edward V. Henry Tudor and his supporters were set to sail to England from Brittany to aid the rebellion, but a severe storm forced them to turn back. The rebellion failed, but Henry's time was coming.

Soon enough, he would unite the Houses of York and Lancaster and start the reign of the Tudor dynasty.

Before that could happen, he would need to assemble an army large enough to invade England. This he could not do in Brittany. Although Duke Francis had supported Henry and provided him with ships for the previous rebellion against Richard's rule, Henry's position in Brittany was becoming increasingly insecure. With Francis weakened from ill health, Henry's fate was now in the hands of Francis' advisors, who were not as keen to protect him from Richard. Recognizing the danger he was in, Henry decided to make a dash for freedom.

It was in September of 1484 that Henry Tudor made his way to France on horseback. He successfully crossed the border disguised as a groom. Here, he met up with Jasper before being received by the French king's envoys. The French court greeted the Tudors with open arms, and as Henry and Jasper wintered in France, they were joined by a steady stream of supporters and defectors. The French, who supported Henry as the future king of England, made sure he was armed with supplies and money, as well as the manpower he would need to attempt a second invasion of England.

In the summer of 1485, Henry set sail toward the British Isles, landing at Mill Bay in Wales in early August. He was accompanied by his uncle Jasper and troops from France and Scotland. The small army marched toward England, and as they went, they gathered more and more supporters who were willing to fight for Henry. The Tudors had strong ties to the Welsh, and thanks to his ancestry, Henry was able to gain a lot of support in Wales. By the time he reached England, Henry was in the company of around 5,000 supportive soldiers who wanted him to take the crown from Richard III. Among them was Walter Herbert—a Yorkist and one of the Herbert children that Henry had grown up with. Additionally, Walter's older brother, William, refused to march against Henry and remained neutral during the coming battle between Henry and Richard III.

By mid-August, Richard received the news that Henry was marching toward London to overthrow him. He swiftly rounded up his armies and went to intercept Henry south of the town of Market Bosworth in Leicestershire. Richard divided his men into three different groups that were to be led by the earl of Northumberland, the duke of Norfolk, and himself. His three armies far outnumbered Henry's forces, but that would count for nothing by the end of the battle.

On August 22, 1485, the Battle of Bosworth Field took place. The Yorkist army led by Norfolk started the offensive, but they struggled against Henry's army, which was under the command of the earl of Oxford, an experienced military tactician. After the initial clash, some Yorkist troops even fled the field. King Richard ordered that Northumberland and his men join the battle to assist Norfolk, but the earl did not heed the command. Faced with this insubordination, Richard was forced to come up with a different plan. He decided to have his men charge full strength across the field and go directly for Henry. If they could kill Henry, the fight would be over.

Watching these events from the sideline was Margaret's husband, Thomas Stanley. He and his younger brother had come to the field at Bosworth with an army of their own.

They had not engaged yet and stood unmoving in a neutral position between the two armies. King Richard had suspected for some time that the Stanleys had defected from his side to support Henry Tudor. Thus, in an effort to secure his loyalty during this crucial battle, Richard had taken Thomas Stanley's eldest son hostage. Thomas, however, had given only a torpid response to the threat: "Sire, I have other sons."

And so, when Richard ordered the all-out charge and the Stanleys saw that Richard's knights were separated from the rest of his army, they took the opportunity to swiftly surround and kill the king. As news of Richard's death spread across the battlefield, the Yorkist forces disintegrated. Henry, and the Lancastrians, had won. Directly following the battle, it was Thomas Stanley who first placed the crown on Henry's head, crowning him as the king of England on August 22, 1485. His crowning took place under an oak tree not far from the battlefield where he had successfully fought for the throne.

The Battle of Bosworth Field was the last major battle of the Wars of the Roses and effectively ended the civil wars which had raged in England for the past three decades. Henry's victory at Bosworth marks the end of the Plantagenet dynasty and the Middle Ages in England, making it one of the defining moments in English history. England now saw the rise of the Tudor dynasty and the advent of the modern era.

Chapter Three

The Tudor Dynasty Begins

"Then Henry the Seventh liberated the land by divine and human right, with divine power vindicating, willing, and assisting, as from a most brutal enemy. He swiftly overcame and slaughtered Richard as he deserved and drove tyranny from the island. After the death of Richard, which please the whole kingdom, he began his reign in the year 1485."

—Bernard André

After his victory at Bosworth, Henry made his way to London where the date of his official coronation ceremony was set for October 30, 1485. Henry made sure to date his reign from August 21, the day before the battle at Bosworth, a decision which conveniently enabled him to label his opposers as traitors and confiscate Richard III's property and lands.

It was essential for Henry to secure his hold on the throne and win the favor of commoners and nobility alike. He wanted his defeat of Richard III to be seen as the beginning of a new era for England rather than a continuation of the Wars of the Roses. Thus, Henry hired chroniclers to write about his reign in a good light. Henry told them to communicate to the public that his victory at the Battle of Bosworth Field was one where good had triumphed over evil. The chroniclers were to make the people of England see that the beginning of the Tudor dynasty was synonymous with a fresh start for the country. And it seemed to work—for the next three centuries, the Battle of Bosworth Field was painted as a glamorous victory where the good forces had taken out the evil ones.

No expense was spared in the effort of portraying Henry VII as a worthy successor rather than yet another interloper. Henry's official coronation ceremony in October was made a grand affair worthy of any king. Present at the ceremony were Henry's dear uncle, Jasper Tudor, and his stepfather, Thomas Stanley, who had performed the first unofficial coronation of Henry after the battle. Henry's mother, Margaret, was perhaps most pleased of all to finally see her now 28-year-old son on the throne. According to eyewitnesses, she "wept marvelously" when the crown was placed on her son's head.

After Henry was made king, he and Margaret seemed to make up for lost time. Throughout Henry's reign, Margaret was treated almost like a queen and dressed only in the most exquisite garments. She remained by Henry's side as one of his most trusted advisors, and her manor at Collyweston would come to serve as a base for the crown in the East Midlands. But, of course, it was also time for Henry to marry and give England a proper queen.

At Henry's first Parliament meeting, the speaker requested that the king's "royal highness should take to himself that illustrious lady Elizabeth, daughter of King Edward IV, as his wife and consort; whereby, by God's grace, many hope to see the propagation of offspring from the stock of kings, to comfort the whole realm." Henry agreed. He had already sworn an oath to marry Elizabeth, and everyone's hope was that this unification of Henry, a Lancastrian, and Elizabeth, a Yorkist, would put a definite end to the civil wars. With this in mind, Henry's royal emblem was created by combining the Red Rose of Lancaster and the White Rose of York. This Tudor Rose signified that the Tudor dynasty ended the Wars of the Roses through the unification of the Houses of Lancaster and York. Contemporary writer and poet Bernard André summed it up perfectly when he wrote, "It was decreed by harmonious consent that one house would be made from two families that had once striven in mortal hatred."

Henry and Elizabeth were married on January 18, 1486, at Westminster Abbey. The wedding was celebrated in the customary fashion with lavish gifts, feasts, dances, and tournaments. Although their marriage was one of political convenience, Henry and Elizabeth appeared to have grown to love each other. Elizabeth was described as beautiful, gentle, and kind; she did not exercise much political influence—that role was reserved for Henry's mother, Margaret—but she enjoyed a quiet life with her servants at Eltham Palace. Henry and Elizabeth would be blessed with many children. Shortly after the wedding, Elizabeth became pregnant with their first child, a son named Arthur, who was born in September of 1486. Arthur was followed by seven more children, four of whom survived infancy: Margaret, Henry, Elizabeth, and Mary.

These children were crucial to secure both Henry's place on the throne and the future line of succession. Still, Henry knew that he would face threats from others with a claim to the throne. He did his best to account for these threats and take steps to prevent rebellions involving any of the potential rivals he may have had. He even went so far as to have the ten-year-old earl of Warwick, Edward, arrested and imprisoned in the Tower of London. Because of his Plantagenet blood, Edward was kept imprisoned for 14 years until his escape in 1499. Edward would not enjoy freedom for long, however, as he was executed later that same year. Upon his death, the House of Plantagenet became extinct in the legitimate male line.

Although Henry did his very best to prevent opposition to his rule, the outbreak of rebellions seemed inevitable in fifteenth-century England. Already in his first year as king, Henry faced the first out of a number of armed uprisings: the Stafford and Lovell rebellion.

The instigators of this rebellion, Viscount Lovell and Humphrey Stafford, had participated in the Battle of Bosworth Field as supporters of Richard III. After the battle, they had gone into hiding at Colchester Abbey. Since that time, they had been conspiring to overthrow the king to bring the Yorkists back in power. Always vigilant to any threat to his power, Henry had stationed spies all over England who monitored known supporters of his predecessors. In April of 1486, Henry got word that Lovell and Stafford were plotting against him from their hideout in Colchester Abbey. The king sent two men, Sir William Tyler and Sir Richard Edgcumbe, to arrest them. Lovell managed to flee the area and found new sanctuary with Margaret of York in Flanders. Humphrey Stafford and his brother, meanwhile, went on to Worcester where they instigated a rebellion. They had not selected the greatest place to start their uprising, however, as Henry VII had many supporters in that region.

When Henry heard what had happened, he decided to go to Worcester to shut the rebellion down for good. The brothers got word that the king was headed their way and quickly sought sanctuary again, at Culham Abbey this time. Here, the brothers were immune to arrest—or so they thought. On May 14, the Stafford brothers were removed from Culham Abbey by force on the orders of the king. They were then ushered to trial where they were found guilty of treason. The arrest of the Stafford brothers instigated a series of protests because of Henry's violation of sanctuary, but in the end, the Court of King's Bench ruled that their removal from sanctuary at Culham Abbey was lawful and that the laws of sanctuary should not be applicable in cases of treason. Henry then ordered the execution of Humphrey Stafford; his younger brother Thomas was given a pardon.

The Stafford and Lovell rebellion was just one in a series of rebellions that Henry would face throughout his reign. The following year, the Yorkists tried again to depose Henry. This time, their leader was the earl of Lincoln. Lincoln and his Yorkist supporters were rallying behind Lambert Simnel, a boy who was claimed to be Edward, the earl of Warwick. The real Edward had disappeared from public view a couple of years back when Henry had him imprisoned in the Tower of London. Thanks to Simnel's resemblance to Edward, Lincoln was able to promote him as the true Yorkist heir.

The rebellion first broke out in Dublin, Ireland where Lincoln had Simnel crowned as "Edward VI" in May of

1487. Lincoln then rounded up around 4,500 men, mostly Irish mercenaries, to invade England and depose Henry VII. The army made landfall in Lancashire on June 4. Others met up with them upon their landing, and in total, their numbers grew to more than 8,000 men. Lincoln's men marched through the region, traveling two hundred miles in just five days. When they got to Bramham Moor just outside of Tadcaster, some 2,000 Yorkists attacked and defeated a small force of Lancastrians.

Lincoln's army was able to defeat several smaller forces of the royal army, but because they had to split up and battle Henry's men in different places, the Yorkists were delayed in their advance. The lull in advancement allowed Henry to bring in more help. With the addition of these forces, Henry's army was much larger than that of the Yorkists, and they also had more provisions and weapons. Now ready for a final battle, Henry and his men started off toward Newark on June 15.

Henry and Lincoln's encounter on June 16, which became known as the Battle of Stoke Field, is considered by some the last battle of the Wars of the Roses. This battle between around 8,000 Yorkist forces and 12,000 Tudor (Lancastrian) forces was even larger than the Battle of Bosworth Field. Henry's army was led by the earl of Oxford, the trusted commander who had brought Henry to victory during the Battle of Bosworth Field. Oxford split the men into three different units. He then gave the order to send a volley of arrows into the Yorkist army, which was assembled in a single block. That resulted in the rebels giving up the high ground and breaking into an all-out attack. Their hope was that they could push Henry's army back on itself, and because Henry's army was split into units, the Yorkists outnumbered the group that was engaged in the fight at that moment.

Oxford's unit did take a big hit, but they were backed up by highly experienced archers under the command of Jasper Tudor. The Yorkists could not break through Henry's lines with the volleys of arrows that kept raining down on them from the sky. Their lack of body armor made it easy for the archers to cut them down in unending numbers. Once it was clear to Lincoln and his men that they were not going to win this fight, they sought to retreat. However, retreat was not an option because of the River Trent which surrounded them on three sides. Casualties were heavy, and almost all leading Yorkists were killed. Many of the men ended up sliding down a ravine (which became known locally as the Bloody Gutter) to try and escape but ended up cornered and killed like the rest of the army. Henry VII had triumphed.

Following the battle, Henry recognized that the young Lambert Simnel was not to blame for the uprising; he was merely a pawn to the Yorkist instigators. Thus, Henry pardoned Simnel and offered him employment in the royal kitchen. Along with Simnel, the king also pardoned many of the Irish nobles that had supported the rebellion. He would need their help to govern Ireland effectively, and this act of clemency would hopefully win him some support in that area.

Henry protected his seat on the throne quite well, but it was something that he had to pay attention to throughout his reign. He had married Elizabeth of York as a symbol of unification to try to deter the Yorkists from overthrowing him, and although it had worked to some extent, the king had to stay on guard almost to the point of paranoia. Sure enough, not long after Simnel had been dealt with, another pretender would emerge to challenge Henry's rule. This one would be a nuisance for the king for many years to come.

Chapter Four
England and Spain Join Forces

"If I have such good speed and success as I wish, according to your desire, I shall ever be most forward to remember and wholly requite this your great and moving loving kindness in my just quarrel."

—Henry VII

Ever since Henry's first son, Arthur, was born in 1486, talk about his marriage prospects had run rampant in the English court. Royal marriages were at the time the principal way of forming strong alliances, and Henry saw his eldest son's betrothal as a means of further strengthening the Tudor claim to the throne.

Starting in 1487, Henry engaged in discussions with the rulers of Spain, Ferdinand II of Aragon and Isabella I of Castile. They had a daughter who was almost the same age as Arthur, and Henry looked favorably upon a possible union between this Spanish princess and his son. Through this marriage alliance, Henry hoped to gain the acceptance and support of a major foreign powerhouse. The Spanish monarchs, for their part, were promised military help in the event that they went to war against France.

Their agreement was made official in March of 1489 in the form of the Treaty of Medina del Campo. The treaty was to do three major things for England and Spain. First, there would be a common policy laid out for both countries on how to deal with France. Second, there was to be a reduction of tariffs between England and Spain. And finally, there would be a marriage between Arthur Tudor and Catherine of Aragon. Spanish representatives signed the treaty on March 27, 1489, but Henry waited to ratify the treaty until September of the following year.

Shortly after this, a new threat to Henry's authority emerged in Ireland. Just as had happened with Lambert Simnel a few years earlier, an impostor was put forward to challenge Henry's place on the throne. This time, the young man's name was Pierrechon de Werbecque, better known as Perkin Warbeck. He claimed to be Richard, the son of Edward IV and one of the two brothers who had been imprisoned and most likely killed in the Tower of London by Richard III.

After gathering some measure of support in Ireland, Warbeck quickly found his way to France where he was brought into the protection of the French king, Charles VIII. Ever since the outbreak of the Wars of the Roses, foreign rulers had recognized the value in harboring alternative claimants to the English crown. Henry, however, saw France's choice to protect this potential usurper as nothing short of a proclamation of war. He quickly gathered a substantial army and sailed to the French coast in late September of 1492. There, Henry laid siege to the nearest town of importance, Boulogne, to pressure the French into handing over Warbeck.

The French king, not wanting to reignite the Hundred Years' War, quickly backed down and agreed to sign a peace treaty which became known as the Treaty of Étaples. By signing this, Charles agreed to stop assisting pretenders to the English throne and also to pay the English a substantial indemnity for their war expenses. In return, Henry would withdraw his forces from France and stay out of Charles' business in Brittany (one of Charles' main goals as king was to annex Brittany and make it a part of France).

Perkin Warbeck would not be so easily thwarted, however, and when it became clear that he was no longer safe in France, he moved on to find new supporters in mainland Europe. He made his way to the Netherlands and the person who was at the center of anti-Tudor sentiment at the time: Margaret of York. Margaret of York was Edward IV's sister, and she embraced Warbeck as her nephew even though she was most likely aware that he was a fraud. Margaret of York had never accepted Henry's right to rule, and she was willing to overlook the fact that Warbeck, being an impostor, had even less right to rule if it meant that she could depose Henry.

With Margaret of York busy building support for Warbeck in mainland Europe, Henry did everything in his power to prevent another rebellion in England. He sent spies to gather information about the plot surrounding Warbeck and placed the English ports under tight surveillance in the event of an impending invasion. Yet the biggest threat to his rule would come from the very inner circle of the royal family. William Stanley, the brother of Thomas Stanley who had first placed the crown on Henry's head, was overheard saying that "he would never take up arms against the young man, if he knew for certain that he was indeed the son of Edward."

Henry was stunned when he received the news of this potential traitor in his midst. He decided to deal with the matter swiftly. In January of 1495, William Stanley was put on trial and found guilty. Two weeks later, he was beheaded. But the danger was not over yet. In July, Henry's coastal defenses would come to good use when they repelled an attempted invasion at Deal, in Kent. Warbeck, defeated but still at large, next sought refuge in Scotland. James IV, king of Scots, took Warbeck under his wing, and in September 1496, the Scots crossed the border into England to attempt an invasion on Warbeck's behalf. This achieved little more than to enrage Henry, and James IV, recognizing the danger of an imminent English invasion of Scotland, withdrew his support of Warbeck.

Warbeck mounted his final attempt at overthrowing Henry in 1497 when he landed in Cornwall backed by a few thousand men. This rebellion was quickly put down, and a few weeks later, Warbeck was finally captured. Initially, Henry was willing to pardon Warbeck just as he had Simnel. After Warbeck gave a full confession of his true identity, he was offered a place in the royal court. Warbeck would not prove as well behaved as Simnel had been though, and in 1498, he was imprisoned in the Tower of London after having attempted to abscond from the royal court. The following year, he would be executed by hanging after yet another escape attempt.

With the last threat to his authority finally and definitely dealt with, Henry could look forward to more tranquil times. In 1501, the 15-year-old Spanish princess, Catherine of Aragon, arrived at the south coast of England. Catherine had already been married to Arthur by proxy, but now she was finally here in the flesh to play her part in the continuation of the Tudor dynasty. In November of 1501, Prince Arthur and Catherine were wed at St. Paul's Cathedral in London in front of an overjoyed crowd.

Their happiness would not last for long though, as Arthur passed away mere months later in April of 1502. Only 15 years old, Arthur succumbed to disease, likely from a form of tuberculosis or what was known at the time as the English sweating sickness. The king, who rarely showed much emotion in public, surprised his servants when he burst out in tears at the news of his son's death. His grief would only grow worse when his dear wife and queen, Elizabeth, died in childbirth the very next year. Again, the king was beset with sadness and shut himself in his quarters for several days.

The Tudor dynasty, for which Henry had fought so hard, looked less and less secure by the day. All hope was now placed on Henry's sole surviving son. If anything were to happen to him, the future of the House of Tudor looked very dark indeed.

Chapter Five

The Work of Henry VII

"By Henry VII, the sword of government was sheathed, the remains of the feudal system at last completely swept away, the undue domination of the nobles set aside to make room for the growing influence of the mighty middle class, in which our modern civilization, with its faults and its merits, has established its stronghold."

—W. Campbell

Whether or not Henry VII was a good king has been the subject of discussion amongst scholars for centuries. What appears certain is that Henry was both determined and intelligent—two traits that led him to success in many of his endeavors. Some of these endeavors would benefit and change England for years to come, and remnants of his accomplishments can still be seen today.

One of Henry's main goals as king was to restore the English economy, which had been depressed during most of the fifteenth century. This he achieved by trade deals, increased taxation, and staying out of expensive wars.

Early on in his reign, Henry entered into the alum trade. Alum was a very valuable commodity in Europe as it was used in the processing of wool and cloth, and it was initially only mined in one small region in Tolfa, Italy. The Pope controlled this region, and therefore alum was an important source of income for the papacy. Henry, wanting to secure a role for England in the alum trade industry, started licensing ships that would source alum from another region: the Ottoman Empire. By importing alum from the Ottoman Empire, Henry was able to offer it to buyers in England and the Low Countries at a much lower cost than the Pope. This enterprising idea did cause a bit of conflict between Henry and Pope Julius II as Tolfa had been the sole provider of alum for many years, but it would be worth it in the end. Through this new source of income, Henry was able to refill the previously empty royal coffers.

Henry also elevated England's trade stance by subsidizing the shipbuilding industry in his country. Doing that not only opened up England to better trade, but it also made the English Navy stronger. In 1495, Henry commissioned Europe's very first dry dock at Portsmouth. It remains to this day as the world's oldest surviving dry dock.

Another success came with an agreement that Henry made in 1496 with the Netherlands. Two years prior to that, Henry had banned trade, specifically in wool, with the Netherlands because of their support of Perkin Warbeck. Henry imposed a trade embargo to show other countries that going against him and showing support for his opposers would not be tolerated and would be to their detriment. In response to the ban, the only company producing Flemish wool moved its operation from Antwerp to Calais, France. England also kicked any merchants from the Netherlands out of the country.

After some time had passed, the government of the Netherlands could see that this trade conflict was severely hurting their economy. Henry took this opportunity to propose the Magnus Intercursus, or the "great agreement," as a deal between England and the Netherlands that did away with the taxation on goods of English merchants. This deal, which was very favorable to England, brought with it a lot of wealth for Henry and his kingdom upon its implementation in 1496.

Taxation was another key source of income in Henry's quest to bring back wealth to the monarchy. Early on, Henry tasked his lord chancellor, Archbishop John Morton, with developing a new, more effective tax policy. Morton's take on tax collection was simple: no-one was to be exempted. He once stated that, "If the subject is seen to live frugally, tell him because he is clearly a money saver of great ability, he can afford to give generously to the King. If, however, the subject lives a life of great extravagance, tell him he, too, can afford to give largely, the proof of his opulence being evident in his expenditure." Morton's reasoning on the subject meant that no-one could get out of paying taxes—a policy which greatly benefited the English government.

All of Henry's work was geared toward re-establishing the authority of the throne. England had been through so much in the past years, and respect for the monarchy had all but disappeared by the time Henry took the crown. The nobility was out of control and had way too much power, so Henry did all he could to bring everyone into line. If nobles could prove their loyalty to the king, Henry allowed them to exert some power in their respective regions. For those that he saw as threats, however, he issued proclamations and new laws that stripped them of some of their power and wealth. To avoid rebellions, Henry limited the nobility's ability to keep large private armies by enacting laws against livery and maintenance. If nobles were found to break these laws, they were liable to pay heavy fines to the crown, which further diminished their influence.

Yet Henry's most significant means of control was what he called the Court of Star Chamber. The court, which was held at the Palace of Westminster, consisted of members of the Privy Council and common-law judges. The point of the Star Chamber was to provide additional governance over prominent people in the country. Henry wanted to make sure that if someone of noble stature committed a crime, that person would be dealt with more fairly than they would in the equity and common-law courts. Many times, nobles were pardoned for their crimes based on their status. The establishment of the Court of Star Chamber would change that and help to keep powerful people (and potential threats to the crown) in check.

During his reign, Henry greatly extended the use of Justices of the Peace. These justices, who were appointed on a yearly basis, held the power to enforce the laws of the assigned shire they presided over. They also served to counteract some of the corruption which ran rampant in fifteenth-century England by, among other things, replacing suspect jurors in trials. But as was customary with Henry, he kept the justices on a short leash. No-one was to be more powerful than the king.

Chapter Six
Late Life and Death

"If it be true that England showed a greatness and a marked flowering of her spirit and genius in the course of the sixteenth century, such a development would have been inconceivable without the intermediation of Henry of Richmond's regime."

—Stanley Bertram Chrimes

In the years following the deaths of Henry's son and wife, the king saw a steep decline in his mental and physical wellbeing. The high-spirited man who had once loved to entertain himself and his guests with hunting, games, gambling, dances, and plays now spent most of his time alone, glumly and joylessly ruling the prosperous kingdom he had created. The English people and nobles had no love for their king and, disregarding the fact that Henry had managed to create peace and stability in the realm, saw him merely as a miser who greedily counted his money in solitude. Gone were the days when Henry had bestowed lavish gifts upon friends and family; his favorite recipient of his charity, Queen Elizabeth, was dead after all.

Although Henry VII's reputation for greed remains as the most vividly remembered part of his legacy, it is not entirely deserved. Throughout his reign, Henry was not afraid of spending money to impress subjects and foreigners alike. He paid a substantial amount to acquire an eagle and a leopard for the royal zoo and once gave his wife a lion as a New Year's Eve gift. When the king's deer ate a poor peasant's corn harvest, Henry promptly reimbursed him. Although Henry generally kept running costs and salaries low, he was not against giving generous bonuses and rewards to people he thought deserved it. He once paid a chef more than £38 to garnish a salad, and in 1492, he rewarded the jousters that entertained him during a tournament with £132 (a small fortune at the time).

Still, by the time of Arthur and Elizabeth's deaths at the beginning of the sixteenth century, Henry's reputation as a greedy miser only grew. Henry was not overly concerned about this—his main focus was, as it had always been, to secure the Tudor dynasty and the line of succession. With the crown prince dead, Henry's remaining son, Prince Henry, took the place as heir apparent. The king started looking into the possibility of having Arthur's widow, Catherine of Aragon, wed to young Henry. By doing this, the king would be able to maintain the alliance with Spain while also keeping Catherine's substantial dowry in England.

Henry also considered marrying Catherine himself. There was still time for him to have more children, and it was never a bad idea for a king to shore up his succession by begetting a few extra heirs. Therefore, when Henry asked Pope Julius II for papal dispensation for his son to marry Arthur's widow, he made sure also to include himself. Catherine's mother, however, was not so keen on having the 46-year-old king marry her 18-year-old daughter. In an attempt to divert his attention elsewhere, she suggested that her niece, Joanna of Naples, might be a better match. Joanna's husband, the king of Naples, had died a few years earlier, which left Joanna as a childless widower in her twenties.

In 1505, Henry was sufficiently interested to send a few ambassadors to Naples to report on Joanna's qualities as a prospective bride. Most important, he required a detailed description of her appearance: What was the color of her hair? What was the size and shape of her nose? What was the condition of her teeth? Did she have hair on her upper lip? What was the complexion of her skin? He even asked about the size of her breasts and whether her breath was sweet. The king had also provided a description of what he thought a suitable wife should look like, and the description perfectly matched his late wife, Queen Elizabeth.

Henry never did seem to get over Elizabeth. After her death, he stopped using the Tower of London as his royal residence, and future royal births would take place in palaces instead of the Tower. Even though the king kept an eye open for a new potential wife, he would not end up remarrying.

By the spring of 1507, Henry was suffering from recurring bouts of what was most likely tuberculosis. He had an incessant cough and a serious throat infection. Some feared that the king, now 50 years old, was close to death. Over the coming year, he would temporarily recover only to fall ill again. He lost many of his teeth, his hair thinned, he lost weight, and his eyesight deteriorated. Then, in 1508, Henry fell ill with acute rheumatic fever. Even after the fever subsided, he was not given respite, and during the rest of the year, the king was reportedly beset with "chronic fatigue, a loss of appetite and bouts of depression."

When Henry fell seriously ill again in early 1509, it was obvious to everyone that the king's death was coming. Realizing that his time was near, Henry asked to see his confessor in April. The confessor anointed his body with holy oil and administered his last rites. Then Henry kissed the crucifix and asked for his lord to come and take him. But Henry did not pass away that night. The following day, the king used his last hours to speak to his son, the heir apparent who was to be his successor on the throne, reigning as Henry VIII. According to Henry VIII, his father told him that he needed to make good on the alliance between England and Spain and marry Catherine of Aragon, which is what Henry VIII would eventually do. Some of Henry's council members contradicted this version of events, however, and claimed that the dying king told his son that he was "free to marry whom he chose."

In any case, King Henry VII died on the night of April 21, 1509 at Richmond Palace from tuberculosis. The council kept the king's death a secret for two days; then, on the morning of April 24, Henry VIII was crowned as the next king of England. Henry VII was survived by his mother, Margaret Beaufort, and it was she that arranged her son's funeral and burial at Westminster Abbey. Henry would be laid to rest next to his beloved wife, Elizabeth. The two had been the first to unite the Houses of York and Lancaster and would remain forever by each other's side.

The first monarch of the Tudor dynasty had died, but the legacy that Henry VII left behind was only the beginning of what the Tudor family would bring to England.

Conclusion

Henry VII was not destined to be the well-known (or perhaps better described as infamous) king that his son was after him, but his place in history remains important. With his victory over Richard III in 1485, Henry brought England out of the Middle Ages and ushered it into the modern era. His reign ended decades of bloody civil wars and provided the wealth and stability necessary for commerce and art to thrive in England. When Henry's son, Henry VIII, ascended the throne in 1509, it marked England's first uncontested transfer of power in almost 90 years. This fact alone is a testament to Henry's achievements.

With Henry's establishment of the Tudor dynasty, he laid the foundation for the rise of England's golden age under his granddaughter Elizabeth I in 1558. But although many would agree with historian John Guy's statement that "England was economically healthier, more expansive, and more optimistic under the Tudors than at any time since the Roman occupation of Britain," not all changes that the Tudor family brought would be good. This was an era of tumult and challenges, and some Tudor monarchs would prove better equipped to handle their duties than others.

Still, by the end of the Tudor era, England had emerged as a major world power with its formidable Royal Navy. It was with ships that England would build its immense wealth and extend its influence across the globe, eventually resulting in the largest empire the world had ever seen. And it all started with the man who set the stage for England to become a major player, Henry VII.

Printed in Great Britain
by Amazon